TRAVEL PUZZLES

First published in the UK in 2025 by Studio Press,
an imprint of Bonnier Books UK
5th Floor, HYLO, 105 Bunhill Row, London, EC1Y 8LZ

www.bonnierbooks.co.uk

1 3 5 7 9 10 8 6 4 2

ISBN 978-1-83587-118-8

Written by Roland Hall
Edited by Frankie Jones
Designed by Alessandro Susin
Production by Giulia Caparelli

MIX
Paper | Supporting responsible forestry
FSC® C018072

The authorised representative in the EEA is Bonnier Books UK (Ireland) Limited.
Registered office address: Floor 3, Block 3, Miesian Plaza
50–58 Baggot Street Lower,
Dublin 2, D02 Y754, Ireland.
compliance@bonnierbooks.ie

A CIP catalogue record for this book is available from the British Library
Printed and bound in Great Britain by Clays Ltd, Elcograf S.p.A.

Disney

TRAVEL PUZZLES

HOLIDAY ACTIVITIES FOR BRIGHT MINDS

INTRODUCTION

A holiday is a wonderful thing. School is out, work is over and there's time to play, have fun and relax or just do something different. Sometimes you go away, sometimes you stay at home but it's always nice to have a change from the usual.

But after a few days your brain often decides it has had enough rest. A few lie-ins and you are already less tired. A walk on the beach and you feel the benefit of the sea air. A trip to the park and you are ready for more. So how about some exercise for your brain? It likes to explore new places too!

This book has 100 challenges for you and your brain, and you can try them any time when you are on – or even just thinking about – a vacation (or even if you aren't). You can solve these puzzles while you are sitting on a sofa, lolling on lounger or chilling in a car. They provide a great way to pass time when you are waiting in a queue, when you are alone or even with other people.

There are many puzzle types in this book, all with

a theme of holidays and all of them featuring characters from your favourite Disney movies. Some are visual – you will have to look for differences in images. Some are word puzzles, where you must think about your vocabulary or spelling. There are mathematical puzzles – yes, you'll have to add stuff up! And there are also logic puzzles, where your brain will need to work hard to resolve them. There are even a few riddles, designed to make you think outside the box – or the swimming pool, depending on where you are.

Solving puzzles should be a challenge, but above all it should be fun, so if you get stuck on one puzzle just move on to another and come back later. Or ask a friend to help – solving puzzles can be a great group activity.

So, have fun, wherever your holiday takes you, whether that is to a beach, a ski slope, a mountain or just at home in an armchair!

The Puzzles

Puzzle 1

RAYA'S BEACH CROSSING

Sisu the water dragon has become separated from Raya; they are on opposite sides of the beach and Raya wants to walk to her companion so they can talk about their adventures – and plan new ones. Can you help Raya make her way from one side of the beach to the other?

START

FINISH

Puzzle 2

TIANA'S TIME OUT

Tiana dreams that one day she can take a holiday from her two busy jobs... All the words in the list are about a beach-side vacation. Can you find them all?

BEACH
BOOK
BUCKET
FLIPPERS
KAYAK
LAGOON
LIGHTHOUSE
OCEAN
SEASHELL
SNORKEL
SPADE
SURFING
TIDE
TOWEL
WAVES

L	A	G	O	O	N	T	C	E	N
I	R	S	U	R	F	I	N	G	B
G	F	S	E	E	A	D	S	O	U
H	T	L	N	A	T	E	P	C	C
T	E	O	I	O	S	C	A	E	K
H	B	K	W	P	R	H	D	A	E
O	E	A	A	E	P	K	E	N	T
U	A	Y	V	P	L	E	E	L	P
S	C	A	E	A	J	B	R	L	L
E	H	K	S	B	O	O	K	S	C

Puzzle 3

ARIEL'S SUDOKU SECRET

Fill in the grid so that each row, column and 2x2 box contains the numbers 1, 2, 3 and 4 once only. The highlighted number reveals how many friends Ariel is going on holiday with!

			3
	2		
	(highlighted)	1	
2			

Puzzle 4

TOULOUSE IN TIME?

It's getting late and Madame Bonfamille wants to get Toulouse and his siblings home in time for tea and a painting session after their day out. They are 10 kilometres from home and the carriage travels at 20 kilometres per hour. It is 5.40, will they get home in time for tea at 6?

Use this space if you need to work it out on paper.

Puzzle 5

ABUELA'S HOUSE INSPECTION

Abuela Alma needs to step into every room of the Madrigal family house; she wants to make sure everything is clean and tidy before the party can begin. To solve this puzzle you must start at square 1 of the grid and make your way to square 16. You can jump over squares, but you have to follow the direction of the arrows and you may only go through each square once, so plan your route carefully!

1 ↘	↓	↙	↙
↗	↓	↗	↖
↑	→	↑	↑
↗	→	→	16 ¤

Puzzle 6

FIND NEMO'S HOME!

Fill in a word on each rung of this word ladder to take Nemo from LOST to HOME.

To solve this puzzle, you can only change one letter at a time, and each rung must contain a proper word.

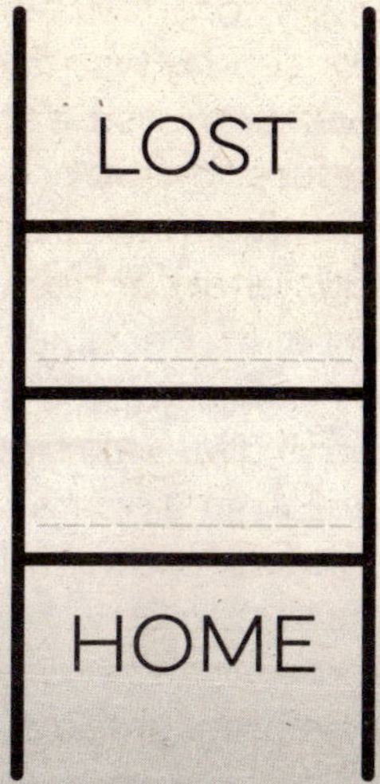

Puzzle 7

SUM SUDOKU WITH SARGE

Each row and column on the grid must contain the numbers 1, 2, 3 and 4 once only.

Additionally, the arithmetic clues must be correct (the number in the top left corner of each thick box must be possible to make from the numbers within each thick box from the arithmetic operation that is shown, for example '5+' must add up to 5).

4x	5+		2÷
	2÷	1-	
5+		(highlighted)	2-
	4x		

The highlighted number shows how many hotel rooms in Molly's dolls' house Sarge has to book in order to take all his troops on holiday!

Puzzle 8

COMPARING POCAHONTAS

When you travel you always need to be observant – that's how you can be sure you won't miss a thing! Fortunately, you can train yourself, and here is a chance to do just that. Pocahontas is pictured here in silhouette, but each one has a small difference from the original. Can you circle each difference in the images below?

1

2

3

4

Puzzle 9

MOANA'S OCEAN MATHEMATICS

In order to navigate the islands and the seas, Moana needs to do some sums before she sets a course for her journey. Can you fill in the grid by doing the calculations required? You may use the numbers between 1 and 9 once only, so be careful!

Cross off the numbers in the chart below as you go:

1	2	3	4	5	6	7	8	9

	+		-	8	=	0
+		-		-		
	+		-		=	5
-		+		+		
1	+		-		=	12
=		=		=		
11		7		9		

Use this space for working out your sums:

Puzzle 10

AURORA'S WAKE-UP CALL

If Aurora wants to make it to her holiday on time, she will have to get up soon. Can you fill in the grid with the words provided in the list? The shaded word is the most important one!

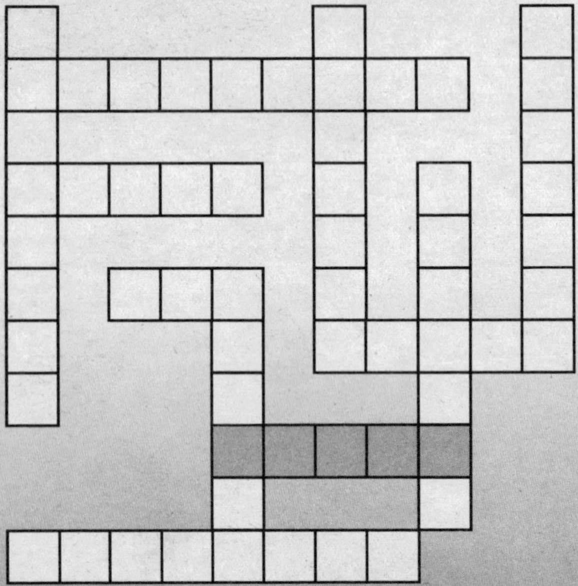

3-letter word
BED

5-letter words
AWAKE
EARLY
SLEEP

6-letter words
DEPART

7-letter words
HOLIDAY
JOURNEY
LUGGAGE

8-letter words
VACATION
PASSPORT

9-letter word
ADVENTURE

Puzzle 11

MINNIE'S DREAM SUITCASE

Minnie loves going on summer holidays, and packs essential items only in her suitcase. For this puzzle, time yourself for one minute while you look at all the objects on this page. Then turn the page and write down or draw as many as you can remember.

How many
did you get?

1–5 Not bad, but you'll need a few more things to really enjoy your holiday!
6–10 That's a good start
11–15 Very good – you won't be missing much
16–20 You are a packing and memory superstar!

Puzzle 12

CINDERELLA'S RIDDLE

A riddle is a fun way to pass some time when you are on a long journey, relaxing on a beach, or even playing with friends. Can you work out the answer to this one?

I love to be at the **ball**, and I always **dance**
In **scarlet** and **black** you'll find me ever
But I will not be there to **jump** or **spring**
And with **gold** and **silver** you'll see me never
For **Cinderella**, I'm always present.
What am I?

Puzzle 13

A DIFFERENT BELLE

Belle is confused. She had a photograph taken while she was visiting a library on holiday, but it doesn't seem quite right. In fact, there are 10 differences between her and the photo. Can you spot all 10 differences between the two images?

Puzzle 14

FRIENDS IN ORDER

Doc, Happy and Sleepy are in the forest, on their way back home after a day of hiking. Can you work out the order they are walking in from the clues below?

Doc is not in front

Happy is not behind Doc

Sleepy is not first or second

______ is at the front

______ is in the middle

______ is at the back

Puzzle 15

EVE'S WORD MATCH

You probably know that EVE likes to tidy things up. Here she is faced with a lot of words that often come in pairs, but they have been separated. Can you help her to match the word pairs together? Each numbered word should be paired with a lettered word.

6. Hot

c. Man

7. Bon

3. Ice

g. Chocolate

4. Sun

a. Spade

1. Suit

h. Cream

b. Fire

8. Surf

2. Bucket

5. Snow

e. Glasses

f. Board

d. Case

Puzzle 16

TEN DISNEY QUESTIONS

Can you answer each of these questions correctly? They are all about travel and other countries.

1. **True or false?** In *Frozen 2*, the Northuldra raise reindeer.

2. What country is Mulan from?
   a. Australia
   b. China
   c. Canada
   d. Spain

3. In *Hercules*, Hades is the ruler of...?
   a. The Dark Place
   b. The Great Middle
   c. The Heavens
   d. The Underworld

4. In *Moana*, what has Te Kā lost?
   a. Her staff
   b. Her hand
   c. Her heart
   d. Her crown

5. In *The Jungle Book*, why does Mowgli have to go to the Man-village?
   a. Shere Khan returned to the jungle
   b. His parents found him
   c. He had an argument with the wolves
   d. He was hungry

6. Where does Miguel journey to in *Coco*?
   a. The Land of the Dead
   b. Mexico
   c. The Between Land
   d. The future

7. Where does *Finding Nemo* take place?
   a. The Great Barrier Reef
   b. Caribbean Sea
   c. Pacific Ocean
   d. Atlantic Ocean

8. Simba can see all the land the light touches when he is standing on...
   a. Pride Rock
   b. Pumbaa's back
   c. Mount Everest
   d. Scar's cliff

9. **True or false?** When Sid Phillips says, 'Yes: I've always wanted to put a spaceman into orbit!', he is referring to Woody.

10. What was the first Disney Park to open?
    a. Disneyland
    b. Disney World
    c. Disneyland Paris
    d. Tokyo Disneyland

Puzzle 17

WORD FINDER BAYMAX

There are a number of words that can be made from the letters of CITY BREAK. Can you help Baymax and Hiro identify the words from the clues below, and fill in the missing letters?

1. A creature you find on the beach: C _ _ _
2. Nice to eat for a treat: _ _ K _
3. A competition to see who is the winner: _ _ C _
4. You may store things in this: _ R _ _ _
5. A very loud noise: _ _ _ K _ _
6. An old boat might be this: _ _ _ _ _ Y
7. People do this, another word for argue: B _ _ _ _ _
8. You wouldn't want to go up stairs that are _ _CK_ _ _
9. Playing golf, you might travel in one of these: _ _ _ T
10. You can build things out of this: B _ _ _ _

Puzzle 18

LIGHTNING'S FAST FILL UP!

Lightning McQueen wants to take a nice, long vacation. To do that he needs to fill up with fuel at the Radiator Springs Garage. You can help him by filling in a word on each rung of this word ladder to take Lightning from FUME to FULL. To solve this puzzle, you can only change one letter at a time, and each rung must contain a proper word.

FUME

_____

_____

_____

FULL

Puzzle 19

MERIDA'S FOREST FOOTPATH

Merida wants to meet up with her brothers as the clan DunBroch is gathering at the Highland games. She needs to get from one side of the forest to the other on her way around the countryside. Can you help her find a safe way across?

START

FINISH

Puzzle 20

JASMINE'S CALCULATIONS

Jasmine is planning a holiday with Aladdin, but needs to do some sums to see if the Magic Carpet can fly that far. Can you fill in the grid by doing the calculations required?

You may use the numbers between 1 and 9 once only, so be careful!

Cross off the numbers in the chart below as you go:

1	2	3	4	5	6	7	8	9

9	-	5	+	3	=	7
+		-		-		
8	+	4	-	2	=	10
-		-		+		
6	-	1	+	7	=	12
=		=		=		
11		0		8		

Use this space for working out your sums:

Puzzle 21

PETER, THE LOST BOYS, AND NUMBERS

Peter and the Lost Boys are playing noisily in a pool, splashing around. Peter comes up with the following test to see if they can solve a sequence puzzle. Can you help them work out the next number in the sequence?

1 2 4 7 11 16 ...

Use this space for working out your sums:

Puzzle 22

SEEING WITH SVEN!

Sometimes you forget things when you are going away, that's why – just like grown-ups say – it's important to make lists! Don't worry though, Sven doesn't make them either and he's the one who has to carry everything for an icy vacation.

Look at the images on this page for one minute and then turn over the page and write down or draw as many items as you can remember.

1–5 Not bad, but you'll need a few more things if you want to avoid the cold!

6–10 That's a good start

11–15 Very good – you won't be missing much on the slopes

16–20 You are a packing and memory superstar!

Puzzle 23

STARFISH AND STONES WITH ALBERTO

Looking at the pretty pebbles at the bottom of the sea, Alberto notices that each one has a starfish next to it – but only one. This makes him think of a puzzle, see if you can solve it.

You must work out precisely where on the grid each starfish is placed. Here are the rules:

- The number next to each row and column tells you the number of starfish that will be found on that row or column.
- No two starfish can be next to each other vertically, horizontally or diagonally.
- It is possible for a starfish to be adjacent to more than one pebble.

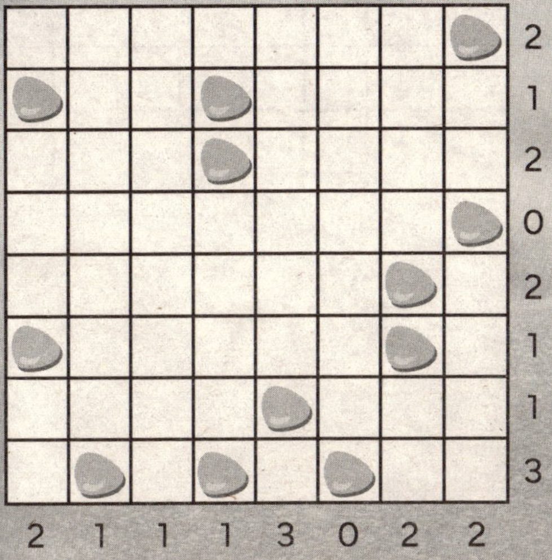

Puzzle 24

ANDY'S ABSENCE PUZZLE

Andy is going away but the toys are not sure if he's going on vacation or for another reason. Can you fill in the grid with the words provided in the list? The shaded word lets everyone know where he is going!

3-letter word
REX

4-letter word
ANDY

5-letter word
LOTSO

7-letter words
COLLEGE
LEAVING

8-letter words
PLAYTIME
TOYSTORY

10-letter words
UNIVERSITY
TRAVELLING

Puzzle 25

RIDDLE ME BAD

Even Mistresses of All Evil need to take a break sometimes. When she was enjoying a cream tea, Maleficent heard this riddle, but she simply cannot work out the answer. She thinks it is some kind of food, but she cannot tell what. Can you figure it out?

Red I am, with heart of stone
Sweet I am, with shiny tone
Round I am, and good to eat
Jam I can be, a teatime treat
What am I?

Puzzle 26

MADRIGAL FAMILY WORDSEARCH

Mirabel Madrigal has plenty to do to help the family prepare for a holiday feast outside under the stars. Can you help her find all the words in the list?

W	S	O	N	G	S	F	O	R	K
S	A	C	H	A	I	R	S	I	O
L	A	T	I	B	Z	Y	D	U	U
C	E	L	E	B	R	A	T	E	T
V	F	M	A	R	O	H	G	E	D
D	A	K	O	D	M	V	R	A	O
R	M	N	S	N	R	E	I	T	O
I	I	I	I	T	A	B	L	E	R
N	L	F	S	G	K	D	L	O	S
K	Y	E	P	L	A	T	E	S	N

CELEBRATE
CHAIRS
DRINK
EAT
FAMILY
FORK
GRILL
KNIFE
LEMONADE
OUTDOORS
PLATES
SALAD
SONGS
TABLE
WATERMELON

Puzzle 27

SWEEPING UP!

If you decide to start casting spells to help you work, you'd better make sure you cast them correctly, unlike this young apprentice, who has created a big problem for himself! A whole lot of brooms are pictured here, but each one has a small difference from the original. Can you circle each change in the images below?

Puzzle 28

WHERE FOR WADE AND EMBER?

Seating arrangements at a special event are always important. When the guests are fire and water elements, they are essential! From the clues given, can you work out who will be sitting next to whom at a square table with one person on each side? Write your answers around the table below.

Ember is opposite Wade

Bernie is not on Ember's left

Brook is on Wade's right

Ember is not next to Wade

Puzzle 29

BO PEEP'S WORD ROUNDUP

Bo Peep is used to looking for her sheep when they run away. This time, they are taking a break so she can have some me-time. She decides to sort out this word jumble, where cities and countries have been scattered all over the place. Can you help her match the correct city with the country it belongs in, as she relaxes?

- Barcelona
- Dublin
- Miami
- Ireland
- Sweden
- Germany
- Rome
- USA
- Cancun
- Marseille
- Hamburg
- Japan
- Scotland
- Italy
- Mexico
- Spain
- Stockholm
- Tokyo
- Edinburgh
- France

Puzzle 30

TEN DISNEY QUESTIONS

Can you answer each of these questions correctly?

1. **Fill in the blank:** In *Beauty and the Beast*, when Belle first reaches the Beast's castle, she finds her father's ___?

2. Who wants to rule the seas?
   a. Ursula
   b. Jafar
   c. King Triton
   d. Captain Hook

3. **True or false?** In *Ratatouille*, Linguini is taught how to cook by a mouse called Marie.

4. In *Up*, Ellie's favourite explorer is ______

5. In *The Lion King*, where does Simba rule?
   a. The Elephant Graveyard
   b. Hakuna Matata Falls
   c. The Pride Lands
   d. All of the above

6. Where does Aladdin find the magic lamp?

7. In *The Emperor's New Groove*, what type of animal is Kronk's best friend, Bucky?
   a. A llama
   b. An elephant
   c. A squirrel
   d. A horse

8. When Miguel sings 'The World Es Mi Familia' at Ernesto de la Cruz's party, why isn't he able to finish the song?
   a. The guitar strings break
   b. Héctor stops him
   c. He falls in the pool
   d. He forgets the words

9. In *The Princess and the Frog*, what happens when human Tiana kisses frog Prince Naveen?
   a. She becomes a princess
   b. He turns back into a human
   c. She turns into a frog
   d. Nothing happens

10. What room in the castle did the Beast give to Belle?
   a. The West Wing
   b. The library
   c. The ballroom
   d. The kitchen

Puzzle 31

WORD FINDER 22

There are a number of words that can be made from the letters of VACATION TIME. Can you help 22 from Soul identify the words from the clues below, and fill in the missing letters?

1. Someone who treats animals: _ _ _
2. A place humans lived many, many years ago: _ _ _ _
3. You bake food in one of these: _ _ _ _
4. The plant on which grapes are grown: _ _ _ _
5. A group of witches: _ _ _ _ _
6. What you watch in a cinema: _ _ _ _ _
7. You get this from the sun: _ _ _ _ _ _ _ D
8. Hopefully you will get one of these, to the ball! _ _ _ _ _ _
9. The country whose capital is Ho Chi Minh City: _ _ _ _ _ _ _
10. When you do nothing on holiday, you are: _ _ _ _ _ _ _ _

Puzzle 32

LUCA'S START CALCULATOR

It's race day and Luca is getting ready to go, but he's lost track of time and isn't sure when the race begins. Fill in the grid so that each row, column and 2x2 box contains the numbers 1, 2, 3 and 4 once only. The number in the shaded box reveals how many minutes Luca has to go until the triathlon starts!

			4
	1	(shaded)	
		2	
1			

Puzzle 33

SUDOKU SUMS WITH WINNIE THE POOH

Winnie the Pooh is going on an expedition to look for more honey! Fill in this grid to find out how many times he walked around the Hundred-Acre Wood on his adventure.

Each row and column on the grid must contain the numbers 1, 2, 3 and 4 once only.

Additionally, the arithmetic clues must be correct (the number in the top left corner of each thick box must be possible to make from the numbers within each thick box from the arithmetic operation that is shown, for example '3+' must add up to 3).

The highlighted number shows how many laps of the forest Winnie the Pooh took!

1-	4+	4x	
		1-	2÷
8x			2-
10+			

Puzzle 34

WORD MATCHING WITH LILO

Lilo is explaining to Stitch what vacations are and what you can do when you are having one. She has two lists of words that often go with each other. Can you help her match the word pairs together? Each numbered word can be paired with a lettered word.

b. Book

6. Read

i. Pizza

8. Build

c. Track

j. Sea

9. Swim

2. Drink

h. Mountain

4. Eat

d. Forest

1. Climb

g. Map

10. Trail

3. Drive

a. Sandcastle

5. Navigate

7. Race

e. Go-kart

f. Lemonade

Puzzle 35

DUMBO DIFFERENCE

Dumbo is confused. He's had a publicity photo taken for his tour, but it doesn't look quite right. In fact, there are 10 differences between the two images. Can you spot all 10 differences between the two?

Puzzle 36

BASIL AND THE CASE OF THE MISSING LETTERS

All of these popular destinations for holidays have had the vowels removed. It looks like you'll need the help of a solving specialist! Can you decipher the strange words and reveal all the destinations? All of the missing letters are listed, so you can check them off as you fill them in.

BR_Z_L	AAIA
GR__C_	AI
_T_LY	AIA
M_L_YS__	EEE
M_X_C_	EIO
S__TH K_R__	IA
S__TH _FR_C_	OU AIA
TH__L_ND	OU OEA
_N_T_D K_NGD_M	UIE AE
_N_T_D ST_T_S	UIE IO

Puzzle 37

FINDING THE INVISIBLE GIRL

The Invisible Girl is, well, invisible. She is trying to get some peace and quiet from the rest of her noisy family. And although she knows where she is, Elastigirl will have to tread carefully to catch up with her unannounced and let her know it's time to pack for vacation.

Starting at square 1, you must move through every room in the house once only on your path to where Violet is hiding in square 16. You must follow the direction of the arrow in each square, but you can jump over squares. Can you work out the path?

1 ↘	↓	←	↙
→	→	↑	↙
↘	←	↓	↑
↑	→	↗	16 ¤

Puzzle 38

QUASIMODO'S SPARROW SEQUENCE

Quasimodo is ringing the bells at Notre Dame to celebrate the holidays. As he does so, he notices groups of sparrows outside in the square in front of the cathedral. They are in numbers that form a pattern. Can you work out what that pattern is, and what the next number will be?

1 2 6

24 ?

Use this space for working out your sums:

Puzzle 39

DESERT WORD FINDER

Simba is alone in the desert and he is deep in thought. All the words in the list below relate to the desert – or do they? They've been muddled up and made into some strange terms. Can you tell what the correct words are?

1. DE SUN (made of sand)
2. C U CATS (plants)
3. SOS AI (place of rest)
4. ARRESTS AHEAD (a famous location)
5. DON SMARTS (something to avoid)
6. MIA REG (Can you believe your eyes?)
7. EL MAC ('The ship of the desert')
8. HURT DOG (no water)
9. SNUB RUN (painful skin)
10. HER FINGERS (a nice drink can be this)

Puzzle 40

BUG PLACEMENT WITH PRINCESS ATTA

Looking at the bugs in a field, Princess Atta notices that each one has a stone next to it – but only one. This makes her think of a puzzle – see if you can solve it.

You must work out precisely where on the grid each bug is placed. Here are the rules:

- The number next to each row and column tells you the number of bugs that will be found on that row or column.
- No two bugs can be next to each other vertically, horizontally or diagonally.
- It is possible for a bug to be adjacent to more than one stone.

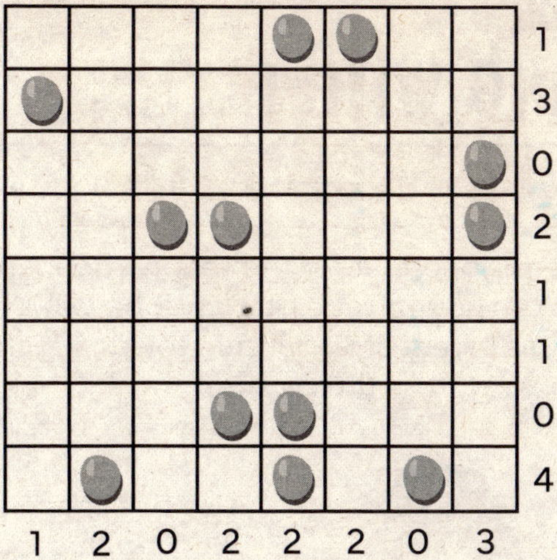
1
3
0
2
1
1
0
4
1 2 0 2 2 2 0 3

Puzzle 41

FLEEING WITH FLYNN

Flynn Rider is fleeing the palace with his loot: a crown. He escapes at six kilometres per hour for the first hour, five kilometres per hour for the second hour and three kilometres per hour after that. How long will it take him to make it to the safety of Rapunzel's tower, which is twenty kilometres away from the palace?

Use this space for working out your sums:

Puzzle 42

MEI'S SUDOKU SHOW

Mei is on her way to watch some live music. Fill in the grid so that each row, column and 3x2 box contains the numbers 1, 2, 3, 4, 5 and 6 once only. The highlighted number reveals the number of members in Mei's favourite band!

	2	5			
4			5		
1		2		3	
	3		2		1
		1			3
			1	2	

Puzzle 43

JUDY'S CROSS-TOWN MAZE

Judy Hopps needs to, well, hop across town from one side of Zootopia to the other in pursuit of a criminal who has stolen Chief Bogo's sunglasses. Can you help her find the quickest way across so she can return the Chief's sunglasses before his holiday?

START
FINISH

Puzzle 44

FELINE DIFFERENCES

Duchess is looking for Berlioz, Marie and Toulouse, who have all run off to play in the sand dunes. Duchess can see some cats who look very similar, but there are a few small differences between them and her kittens. Can you tell the difference between her cats and the others?

Puzzle 45

SEARCH WITH STITCH

Lilo and Stitch are learning travel words. All of the words opposite are spelled out in the word grid, can you help to find them all?

L Q M E T S J H G R R J G X M

U C T G E R M B M E U W J J S

G U R G L X A D A L Z C O E C

G H N U E F C V P A T E U X W

A O I W I T J U E X O D R P H

G T V S I S A Z R L U T N L O

E E Z R L N E W Z S R R E O L

L L T Z P A D B A I I L Y R I

T H F Q K D N F O Y S O T E D

W V F D M C V D W G T I N H A

P H O T O G R A P H K K K C Y

X A E M A B I T I N E R A R Y

M R E S O R T Y B D O S Z K Q

Y S K M V O Y A G E Q P I J L

S O U V E N I R O J Q A E I Z

CRUISE
EXCURSION
EXPLORE
GETAWAY
HOLIDAY
HOTEL
ISLAND
ITINERARY
JOURNEY
LUGGAGE
MAP
PHOTOGRAPH
RELAX
RESORT
SOUVENIR
SPA
TOURIST
TRAVEL
UNWIND
VOYAGE

Puzzle 46

CAPITAL CITY CHALLENGE

Nick Wilde from *Zootopia* is a wise man and has plenty of knowledge of the world and the places in it. In this puzzle, you must match up countries with their capital cities. Be careful: some of them are easier than others, and there are five red herrings!

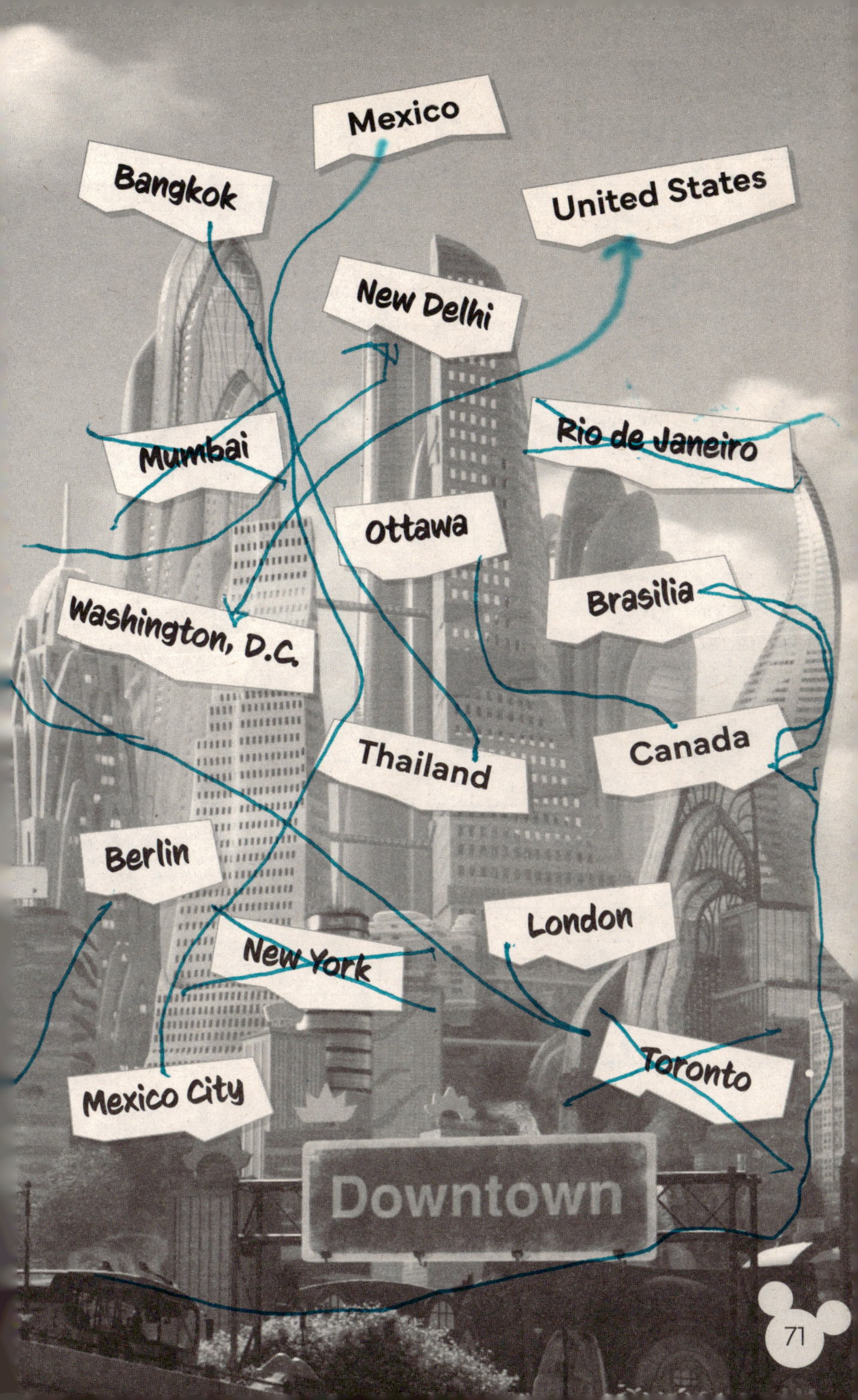

Mexico
Bangkok
United States
New Delhi
Mumbai
Rio de Janeiro
Ottawa
Brasilia
Washington, D.C.
Thailand
Canada
Berlin
London
New York
Toronto
Mexico City
Downtown

Puzzle 47

MEMORIES MAP

Joy would like to take a break, but she has to be sure that all of Riley's memories are stored carefully away, one per rail so they get sent to the correct place. In this puzzle you must work out precisely where on the grid each memory is placed.

Here are the rules:

- The number next to each row and column tells you the number of memories that will be found on that row or column.
- No two memories can be next to each other vertically, horizontally or diagonally.
- It is possible for a memory to be adjacent to more than one rail.

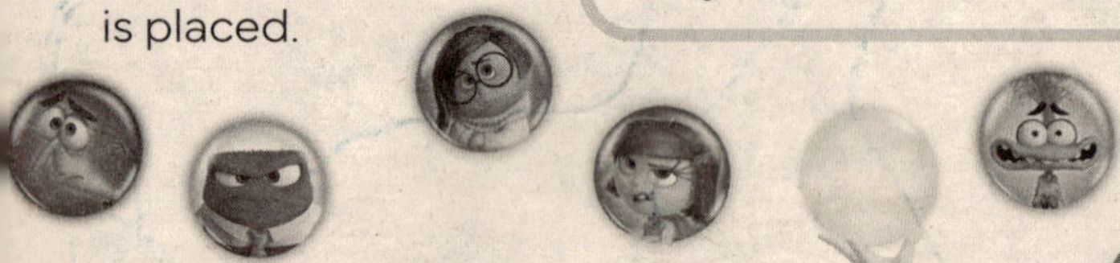

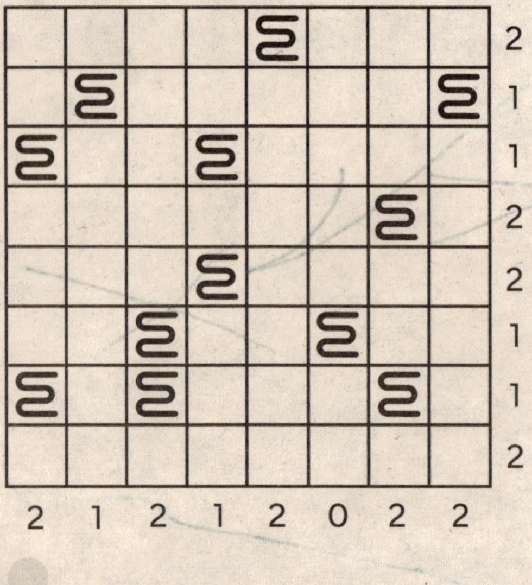

Puzzle 48

MAPPING A MEMORY

Kristoff is puzzling over a map, looking at all the places he'd like to visit on a long trip around the continent. Follow his journey around Europe and try to remember all the places. Then turn the page and write down as many as you can recall.

For an extra challenge, start at Norway and try to remember them all in the correct order.

Use this space to write as many countries as you can remember.

1–5 Not bad, maybe have another go?

6–9 A solid start around the map

10–12 Very good – you didn't miss much

13–15 You are a map and memory superstar!

Puzzle 49

ANGER'S ARITHMETIC SUDOKU

Anger is going to take a well-deserved break!

Each row and column on the grid must contain the numbers 1, 2, 3, 4 once only.

Additionally, the arithmetic clues must be correct (the number in the top left corner of each thick box must be possible to make from the numbers within each thick box from the arithmetic operation that is shown, for example '5+' must add up to 5).

7+	2-		2÷
	2÷	6+	
1-			3x
	12x		

The shaded number shows how many times Anger will blow his top before he leaves on vacation!

Puzzle 50

SILHOUETTE ROUND-UP

Woody is ready for a round-up with Bullseye. They're pictured here with a number of silhouettes, but each one has a small difference from the original. Can you spot each change in the images below?

Puzzle 51

JUST CHECKING THE NUMBERS!

It's the last lesson of the day and Riley is ready to get out and start the holidays with her friends. But first she's got to get past this maths problem: in the square before her, each blank must be filled in by the numbers 1 through 9 once only. All the sums must add up correctly and must be done in order. Can you fill them in?

1 2 3 4 5 6 7 8 9

	+		+		=	12
+		+		-		
	+		-		=	9
-		+		+		
	+		-		=	8
=		=		=		
6		10		7		

Use this space for working out your sums:

Puzzle 52

ANCIENT WORLD MATCHUP

Dinosaurs roamed the world before there were humans, cities and vacations! Arlo is looking at these lists of places, and he knows that each natural wonder belongs with a country. Can you help him to put the two together correctly? Each numbered word matches up with a lettered word.

5. Lake Titicaca
e. Norway
j. Zimbabwe
1. Fjordland
c. Canada
b. Australia
6. Niagara Falls
2. Giant's Causeway
10. Victoria Falls
f. Northern Ireland
3. Grand Canyon
4. Iguazu Falls
a. Argentina

Puzzle 53
CROSSTOWN TRAFFIC

Hiro Hamada needs to get across San Fransokyo in a hurry – he's got a plane to catch if he wants to go on vacation! It's a total distance of 30 kilometres. He has three travel options: can you work out which will get Hiro to the airport first?

1. Go Go Tomago's maglev disks can make him travel at 60 km/h, but they have to be charged for 10 minutes first.
2. Honey Lemon can supply Hiro with some special chem-balls that make his new battle-bot travel twice as fast as normal and carry him too. Its regular speed is 30 km/h.
3. Fred has worked out a crafty shortcut that means he can get Hamada to the airport in only 28 minutes.

Puzzle 54

JOY'S PUZZLED FEELINGS

Joy and the team have nothing to do one day as Riley is reading on the beach. They decide to set each other riddles. Well, Joy decides to ask riddles, the others are not quite so keen... Can you work out the answer to this one?

So many faces I can possess
Sometimes politeness I may transgress
Happiness and anger I do express
I'm activated often by a screen you press
What am I?

Puzzle 55

WHATEVER NEXT!

The trolls are having a snowball fight! They notice that the number of snowballs their opponents have fits a pattern. Can you work out what the pattern is, and what the next number should be?

Use this space for working out your sums:

Puzzle 56

SLING YOUR HOOK

Maui's hook has been hidden under the final one of 16 stones at the bottom of the ocean. In order to get it and not disturb Tamatoa, he's going to have to tiptoe around, and make a path that goes through each square once only. Can you work out what path he should follow, using the arrow indicators to guide you? Note: you must move in the direction of the arrow and go to every square before you reach number 16 and you can jump over squares.

1 ↓	↘	↙	←
↘	↘	↗	↓
↑	←	→	↑
↗	↑	←	16 ¤

Puzzle 57

JASMINE'S JOURNEY

Fill in a word on each rung of this word ladder to take Jasmine from SAND to HOME.
To solve this puzzle, you can only change one letter at a time, and each rung must contain a proper word.

SAND
HOME

Puzzle 58

TEN DISNEY QUESTIONS

Can you answer each of these questions correctly?

1. What item is Cogsworth in the Beast's castle?
2. What is Monsters University's rival school?
3. What Mickey accessory sits on top of the Walt Disney Animation Studios building in Burbank, California?
4. What is the name of Pocahontas's best friend from her tribe?
   a. Kocoum
   b. Winona
   c. Powhatan
   d. Nakoma
5. In which city do the Darling children live in *Peter Pan*?
6. **Fill in the blank:** Moana's island is called _______.
7. In *One Hundred and one Dalmatians*, where do Pongo and Perdita meet?
8. What kind of vehicle do Ian and Barley take on their quest in Onward?
   a. A Pizza Planet truck
   b. A spaceship
   c. A school bus
   d. A van

9. What is the name of the ship where the humans are sent to live in *WALL·E*?

10. In *Up*, what was the name of Charles F. Muntz's airship?

Puzzle 59

URSULA'S LOGICAL SEARCH

Ursula is up to no good in her lair. She is trying to keep tabs on everyone in Atlantica but she has only been given a few clues about some individuals. There are three characters (Sebastian, Flounder and Scuttle), three places (the market, the grotto, the palace), and three objects (a fish, a ship, a trident). Using the clues, can you work out where each character is and what object they have with them?

Use the grid to help you work out the answer by putting a tick next to something you know is correct, and a cross against something you know isn't.

		Places			Objects		
		Market	Grotto	Palace	Trident	Fish	Ship
Names	Sebastian						
	Flounder						
	Scuttle						
Objects	Trident						
	Fish						
	Ship						

Scuttle has the trident.

Flounder is in the market.

Sebastian has the ship.

Scuttle is in the grotto.

Puzzle 60

MONSTER WORD GRID

Mike and Sulley are talking about the good old days at university and putting the words into a grid. Can you help them fit all the words in the correct places? The shaded word is the one they look back on most fondly!

4-letter word
MIKE

5-letter words
SCARE
TEAMS

6-letter words
SCREAM
SULLEY
TALENT

7-letter word
RIVALRY

8-letter word
MONSTERS

10-letter word
RANDY BOGGS

12-letter word
HARDSCRABBLE

Puzzle 61

FROZEN RIVER CROSSING

Anna wants to cross a frozen bay on her journey to visit Elsa for a holiday. Some of the ice is thick enough to walk on but some isn't. Can you trace a safe path across for her? The safe ice flows in a pattern, where each number is added to the next in order to continue. Start at 0 and make your way to the opposite side.

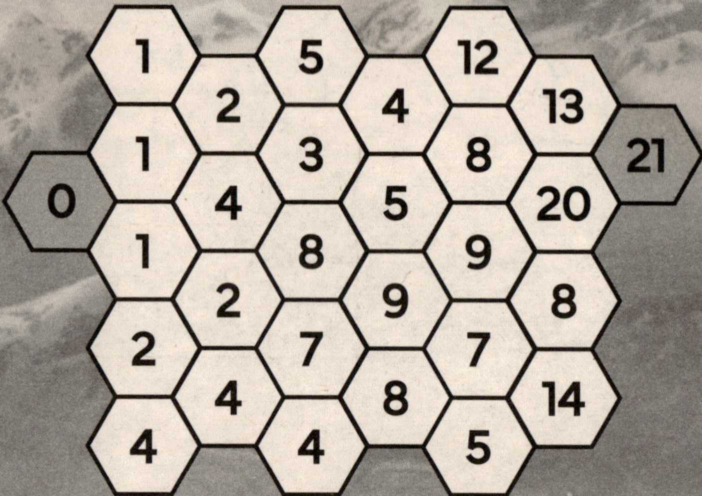

Puzzle 62

LOCKER CODE SUDOKU

Buzz has stored his luggage in a locker at the airport on his way to a vacation but he has unfortunately forgotten the code. Can you help him find it by filling in all the numbers in the grid? Each row, column and 3x2 box must contain the numbers 1, 2, 3, 4, 5, 6 once only.

The code contains the shaded numbers, starting with the number in the top left shaded box and reads clockwise.

5					
6	3				
		1		2	
	2		1		
				6	4
					5

Puzzle 63

DRIVEN TO DISTRACTION

Mater is thinking about what sort of holiday he'd like to take. He's got a big list of words and five categories but they have all got muddled up. Can you help him put the right word with each category? Each category contains three words.

BEACH

MOUNTAIN

THEME PARK

CITY

SAFARI

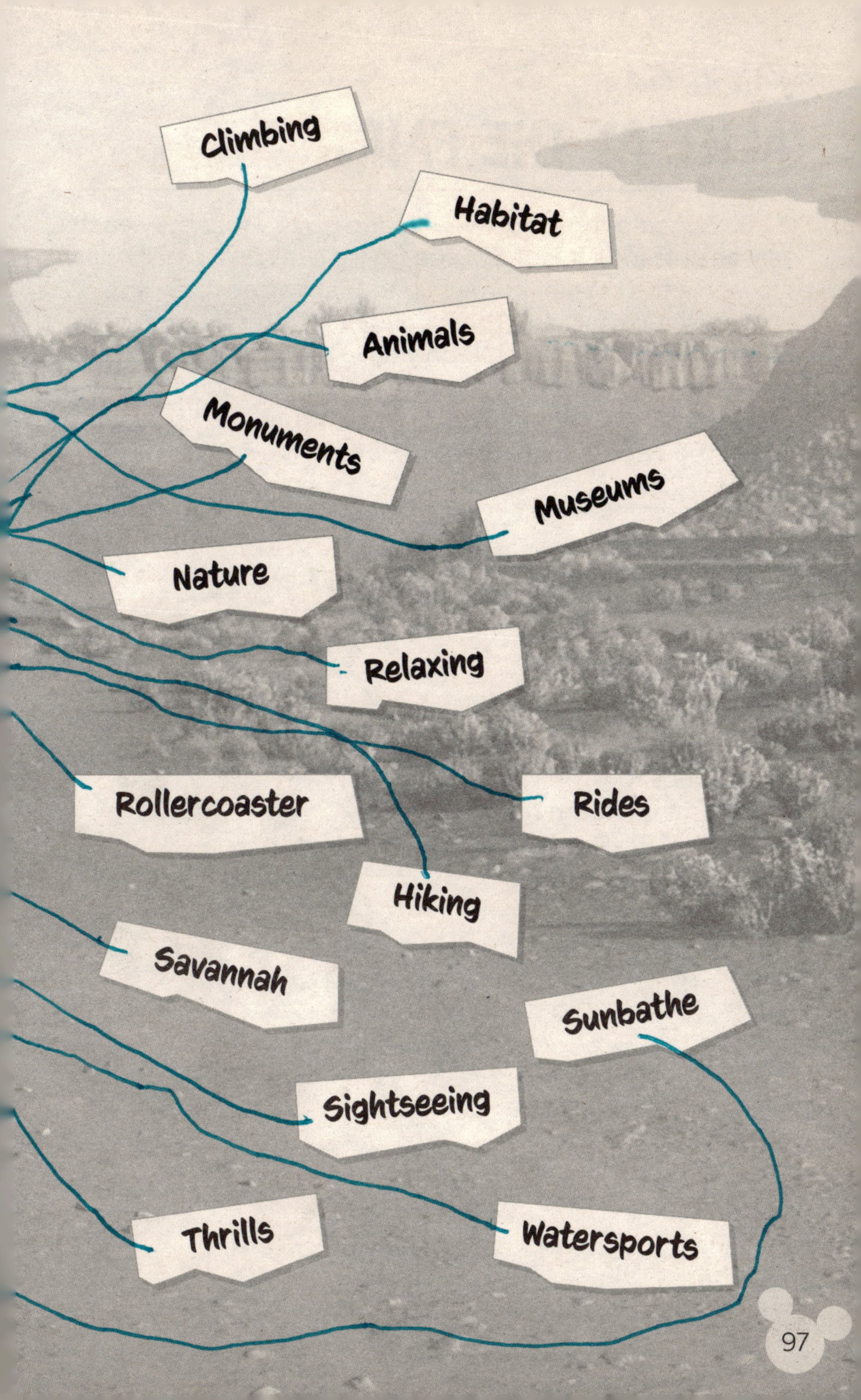
Climbing
Habitat
Animals
Monuments
Museums
Nature
Relaxing
Rollercoaster
Rides
Hiking
Savannah
Sunbathe
Sightseeing
Thrills
Watersports

Puzzle 64

ALICE AT THE FAIR

Alice, Tweedledum and Tweedledee go to a fair. They each pay an entrance fee of £10 and go for a row in a small boat. However, the cashier comes up to them afterwards and apologises, saying that there's a special offer for groups of three and that they should only have been charged £25, so gives them £5 back. They decide to keep £1 each and buy some sweets to share, which cost £2. When they sit down to eat the sweets, Tweedledum does some sums:

They paid £10 each but got £1 each back, so they actually paid £9 each.

Then they paid £2 for the sweets.

£9 times 3 is £27, plus £2 comes to a total of £29, so they seem to have lost £1.

Can you explain where the £1 went? Tweedledum thinks Tweedledee has taken it, Tweedledee thinks Tweedledum has taken it.

Use this space for working out your sums:

Puzzle 65

KRISTOFF'S WARM WORDSEARCH

Kristoff likes to live in a cold country, and has spent some time listing many of the things he likes about it. The words in the list are about a winter vacation. Can you find them all?

```
F R O Z E N X E S C P A C I T
P M M H O T C H O C O L A T E
L Z M I S S Q O K T Y Y B D V
R S X S Z L L J M I I D I I R
G B N D K V K E F D C K N G W
O I S O M A F J I U E T S S S
G K E S W I T P V G R S N N N
G Q L H G M T I L I H K O O O
L C R S L F A T N H V I W W W
E H I L A R C N E G J I B B F
S A G E C O O T Z N C N O A L
N L L D I S Z C D R S G A L A
B E O K E T Y S C A R F R L K
U T O X R U P H X A I I D M E
K P F I R E P L A C E O D H V
```

CABIN
CHALET
COZY
FIREPLACE
FROST
FROZEN
GLACIER
GOGGLES
HOT CHOCOLATE
ICE
IGLOO
MITTENS

SCARF
SKATING
SKIING
SLED
SLEIGH
SNOWBALL
SNOWBOARD
SNOWFLAKE
SNOWMAN

Puzzle 66

OBSERVE THE DIFFERENCE

Bambi and Faline are visiting Thumper for a holiday. Bambi is always alert and looking at what goes on around him. The two images below have 10 differences, can you spot them all?

Puzzle 67

HERCULES' HEAVY PYRAMID

Carrying heavy bags is something Hercules is very good at, so he's a great person to travel with! Can you fill in the missing numbers on this pyramid? The shaded number shows the number of bags Hercules' friends think he can carry!

In a number pyramid each number added to the one next to it makes the number in the box above.

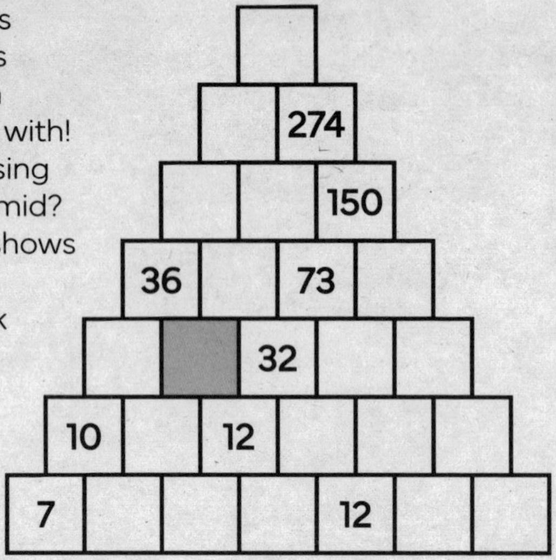

Puzzle 68

THE QUEEN'S CONUNDRUM

The Queen of Hearts has decided to play cards with Alice. However, there's a problem and some of the cards are missing from the deck of 52.

- If she deals cards to three people, there are two cards left over.
- If she deals cards to four people, there are three cards left over.
- If she deals cards to five people, there are two cards left over.

Can you use this information to work out how many cards there are in the pack?

Use this space for working out your sums:

Puzzle 69

SUDOKU WITH SUMS

Prince Charming's servants are packing his royal carriage ready for a holiday.

Each row and column on the grid must contain the numbers 1, 2, 3 and 4 once only.

Additionally, the arithmetic clues must be correct (the number in the top left corner of each thick box must be possible to make from the numbers within each thick box from the arithmetic operation that is shown, for example '5+' must add up to 5).

The highlighted number shows how many bags each of the Prince's servants have to carry for him!

5x	12x	5+		1-
		3-		
3x		6+	1-	
10x				5+
2÷		2-		

Puzzle 70

PUPPY PURSUIT

One of the young Dalmatians has fallen asleep in the house, but it's time to leave for a holiday, and Pongo has gone in to find them. He doesn't know exactly where they are, so he must visit every room in the house in his search for the puppy. Can you guide Pongo from square 1 to square 16? He must pass through each other square once only and follow the direction of the arrows each time, but he can jump over squares.

1 →	↙	↘	↙
→	↗	↓	↓
→	↗	←	↖
→	↑	←	16 ¤

Puzzle 71

TURN UP THE HEAT

FIRE

HEAT

Jack-Jack Parr is not behaving himself with the babysitters – his older brother and sister. In fact, he's become a flaming fireball and is running around the garden! Can you help Violet and Dash turn the word FIRE to HEAT, and hopefully cool him down in the process? Each word on the ladder must change one letter only from the previous one, and must be a real word.

Puzzle 72

GODS OF OLYMPUS

Hercules is on Mount Olympus with Zeus, Hera, Pegasus and Meg. They are sitting down to eat a feast when they realize there must be a seating arrangement to follow.

Hera states, "Zeus is not seated next to me, Pegasus is not seated next to me or Hercules, Hercules is not next to Meg, Meg and I are not next to Zeus. And Hercules should sit to the left of Zeus."

Can you work out where each of them should sit?

Puzzle 73

UNDER SEA SILHOUETTE

When you travel you always need to be observant – that's how you can be sure you won't miss a thing and keep yourself safe. Ursula is pictured here in silhouette, but each new image has a small difference from the original. Can you help Ariel spot each one in the images below?

Puzzle 74

WOODY'S WORD WHEEL

Woody and Buzz are looking for ways to travel to the other side of the country. They've seen a long word that relates to space, and they can find many other words about transport (and other things) using the letters from it.

Can you work out the long word that uses all the letters, and the 10 words there are clues for, opposite?

Then try to find as many other words as you can from the letters.

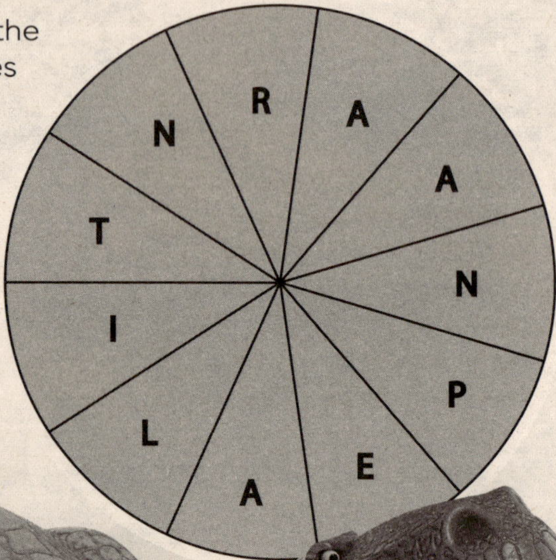

1. Fly in one of these (maybe not you, Buzz!):

_ _ _ _ _ _ _ _

2. You don't want to meet one of these on a boat:

_ _ _ _ _ _

3. Exotic, nocturnal mammal:

_ _ _ _ _

4. A month of the year:

_ _ _ _ _

5. A celestial body:

_ _ _ _ _ _

6. Back to the drawing board:

_ _ _ _ _ _

7. Someone good at art:

_ _ _ _ _ _ _

8. Rail transport:

_ _ _ _ _

9. Jump up:

_ _ _ _

10. A quick sleep:

_ _ _

Puzzle 75
HONEY TIME

Dreaming of pots of honey spread all around the Hundred-Acre Wood, Winnie the Pooh has a puzzle to solve. He wants each pot of honey to have a spoon next to it, but strictly one per pot.

Can you work out where the spoons should go on the grid, using the following rules:

- The number next to each row and column tells you the number of spoons that will be found on that row or column.
- No two spoons can be next to each other vertically, horizontally or diagonally.
- It is possible for a spoon to be adjacent to more than one pot.

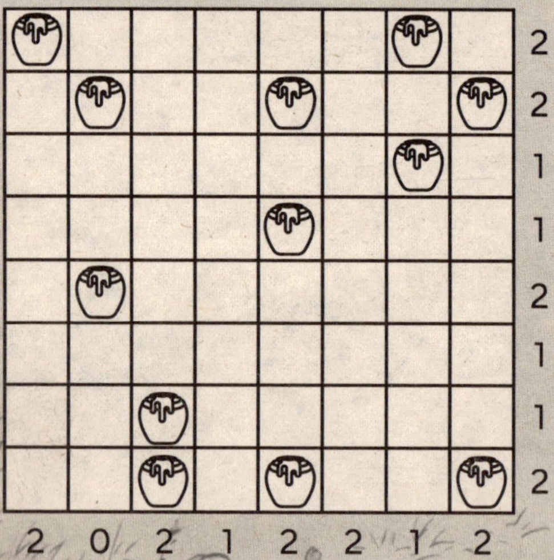

Puzzle 76

MAPPING YOUR MEMORY

Archimedes is a wise bird, and knows his way around the world. Below is a map of South America with a journey plotted on it and the countries marked. Study the journey and the countries for a minute, then turn the page and write down as many as you can remember, in the order of the journey, starting from Brazil.

How many did you get?

1–5 Not bad, maybe have another go?
6–9 Very good – you didn't miss much
10 You are a map and memory superstar!

Puzzle 77

SEALIFE WITH DORY

Dory sees many creatures under the sea on her travels. Can you fit all the creature names into the grid?

5-letter words
SHARK
WHALE

7-letter words
DOLPHIN
OCTOPUS

8-letter words
MANTA RAY
SEAHORSE
SEA OTTER

9-letter words
CLOWNFISH
JELLYFISH

Puzzle 78

WATERY WORD MATCH

Water is a very important element in *Raya and the Last Dragon*. Our planet is more than 70 percent water. Here is a list of some large and significant bodies of water, can you correctly identify which are oceans, which are gulfs and which are seas?

Hint: there are four oceans, ten seas and one gulf!

OCEANS

SEAS

GULF

Caribbean
Pacific
Persian
Black
Atlantic
North
Mediterranean
Sargasso
South China
Caspian
Red
Bering
Yellow
Arctic
Indian

Puzzle 79

TEN DISNEY QUESTIONS

Can you answer each of these questions correctly? They are all about places.

1. In *Fantasia*, where does Chernabog live?

2. In *The Great Mouse Detective*, what country is Bianca from?

3. Where does Joe Gardner live in *Soul*?

4. In *Finding Dory*, where does Dory say she is originally from?

5. Which of the following is not an attraction in Cars Land?
   a. Luigi's Flying Tires
   b. Mater's Junkyard Jamboree
   c. Flo's River Float
   d. Radiator Springs Racers

6. In *Frozen*, where does Elsa create her Ice Palace?

7. Which of the following is not a location in *Coco*?
   a. Plaza de la Cruz
   b. Marigold Grand Central Station
   c. Santa Cecilia Cemetary
   d. Playa de la Muerta

8. In *Cars*, what road leads to Radiator Springs?

9. In *The Lion King*, who rules the Elephant Graveyard?

10. In *The Incredibles*, what is the name of the island Syndrome owns?

Puzzle 80

RIDDLE TIME

Penny is enjoying a day out with Bolt, Rhino and Mittens. She has a riddle for each of them, can you work out what the answers are?

1

What has hands and a face, can tell the time but cannot speak?

2

What is it that starts at the end, ends at the beginning and goes backwards as well as forwards?

3

Lonely I am: I begin eternity, but end time and space,
Curly I am: I start at the end but end every race.
What am I?

Puzzle 81

THE CAVE OF WONDERS

Aladdin is after some treasure. He knows precisely where it is hidden; he just needs to make his way across the Cave of Wonders to pick it up. Unfortunately there are booby-traps everywhere and if he does not follow the exact pathway there will be nothing left by the time he gets there. Can you help him find his way to the treasure that's hidden under square 25? Starting at square 1 you must follow the direction of the arrows and make a path that goes through every single square once only. You may jump over squares.

1 ↘	↙	↙	↙	←
↓	5 ↘	↑	→	↑
↓	↓	↑	↘	←
↘	→	↓	↗	↖
↗	→	→	↖	25 ¤

Puzzle 82

MEDITERRANEAN SPELLING MAZE

Asha is on a journey. Can you help her make her way from the entrance of this maze on the left to the exit on the right? If it is solved correctly, the letters you pass by will spell out the name of an island.

START
A
P
S
O
M
C
S
C
B
Y
E
Z
R
A
I
I
A
B
C
Z
FINISH

Puzzle 83

WORDSEARCH WISHES

Dug the dog is looking forward to a holiday, and he's written down a list that contains lots of the things he likes to do when he's away (it is very similar to what he likes to do at home!). Can you find all of the words in the grid below?

T R E A T A W P A W P R I N T
J B S N I F F I N G N N B S W
O L E I L W A G G I N G S M G
Y W A L K I E S H I K I N G W
R O A D T R I P H G W A T E R
C B S T T R E L A X A T I O N
U E P A F P A D V E N T U R E
D A L S N R L L E X P L O R E
D C G A U D E A J K Z G F P C
L H P O K N C E Y E L N E I T
E B A R K E S A D T M A T C R
S X S O Z X S H S O I P C N A
D O G H O U S E I T M M H I I
D M O U N T A I N N L U E C L
Y T R A V E L Z E F E E H Z S

ADVENTURE	JOY	SANDCASTLE
BARK	LAKES	SNIFFING
BEACH	MOUNTAIN	SUNSHINE
CUDDLES	NAP	TRAILS
DOGHOUSE	PAWPRINT	TRAVEL
EXPLORE	PICNIC	TREAT
FETCH	PLAYTIME	WAGGING
FREEDOM	RELAXATION	WALKIES
HIKING	ROADTRIP	WATER

Puzzle 84

JUNGLE MATHS

Mowgli and Baloo are planning a trip across the jungle. They know they will need to take plenty of food with them so they are adding up how many bananas they'll need. Can you help them fill in the grid, using the numbers 1 to 9 once only?

1 2 3 4 5 6 7 8 9

	+		-		=	6
+		+		-		
	+		-		=	0
-		-		+		
	+		-		=	7
=		=		=		
2		5		10		

Use this space for working out your sums:

Puzzle 85

WALL•E WORDS

EVE travels a long way to Earth where she meets WALL·E, who has been there for centuries, tidying up. The humans left, evacuated from the toxic planet, would like to return at some point. How much do you know about WALL·E?

1. What does WALL·E stand for?

   ____

2. How many robots are still functioning on Earth?

   ____

3. What does EVE stand for?

   ____

4. What is WALL·E's companion on Earth?

5. In what century does WALL·E take place?

6. What important find does WALL·E show EVE?

7. Who saves WALL·E and EVE from being ejected from the ship?

8. What is the name of the captain of that ship?

9. What is the name of the AI that pilots the ship?

Puzzle 86

WORK WORD LADDER

WORK

PLAY

Mike and Sulley enjoy their work, but they also have fun when it's time to play. Fill in a word on each rung of this word ladder to help take the pair from WORK to PLAY.

To solve this puzzle, you can only change one letter at a time, and each rung must contain a proper word.

Puzzle 87

DOG GONE

Cruella De Vil certainly lives up to her name. She has taken one of the Dalmatians! This page shows a lot of different dogs. Study it for one minute and then turn over to the next page, where one dog has been removed. Your challenge is to identify which one has gone!

Puzzle 88

WHERE ON EARTH?

Pinocchio is looking at various places that are popular for winter holidays around the world. Unfortunately someone has removed the vowels from the list, making it very hard to read. Can you help him to work out the correct names?

ASPN (USA)
BNFF (Canada)
CHMNX (France)
CNRY SLNDS (Spain)
MNT FJ (Japan)
RYKJVK (Iceland)
TLLNN (Estonia)
TRMS (Norway)
WHSTLR (Canada)
ZRMTT (Swizerland)

AE
EAI
EA
OU UI
A
IE
AOI
OO
AI
AA IA

Puzzle 89

LOGICAL EMOTIONS

With Riley relaxing on holiday, the emotions are able to take it easy for a bit. Joy, Disgust and Anxiety have come to work and are talking about their dream destinations. Can you work out who wants to go where, and in what order they arrived? Use the grid opposite to mark what you learn from the clues and then use logic to work out the answers.

Joy wants to go to Hawaii

Disgust doesn't want to go to New York

The emotion who arrived first wants to go to Hawaii

The emotion who wants to go to New York arrived second

		Destination			Arrived		
		Alaska	Hawaii	New York	First	Second	Third
Names	Joy						
	Anxiety						
	Disgust						
Arrived	First						
	Second						
	Third						

Puzzle 90

JIGSAW PUZZLER

Flik and Atta are planning a trip to see P.T. Flea and the Circus Bugs. For something to do on the journey, Flik has made an image of them together into a jigsaw puzzle for Princess Atta... but one of the pieces doesn't fit. Can you work out which is the rogue piece?

Puzzle 91

COCO CROSSWORD

Miguel from Coco celebrates *días de los muertos* with his family in Mexico every year. Can you match the words to the blank grid below?

6-letter words

FAMILY

GUITAR

HECTOR

IMELDA

MEXICO

7-letter words

CONCERT

ERNESTO

OFRENDA

SINGING

9-letter word

RELATIVES

10-letter words and phrase

PHOTOGRAPH

REMEMBER ME

12-letter phrase

DAY OF THE DEAD

Puzzle 92

SUDOKU REVEALER

Jessie is helping to organise the toys as they prepare to go on vacation. If you fill in all the numbers in the grid with the simple rule below, you can add up the numbers in the shaded boxes to reveal how many toys are going with Jessie.

5						8		3
8					4		6	
		9	8				4	2
2			4		1			
3								4
			3		7			9
6	5				9	4		
	4		1					8
9		2						5

Each row, column and 3x3 box must contain the numbers 1 through 9 once only.

Puzzle 93

MAGIC MIRROR JUMBLE

This list of vacation-related words and terms has become muddled up: half of the word is the right way round, the other half has been reversed, by the Magic Mirror. Can you figure out what they say, and put the correct word pairs together?

SUN	TRIP
SUIT	CASE
LUG	GUARD
BACK	PACK
RUCK	SACK
PASS	PORT
SEA	CREAM
AERO	SIDE
LIFE	PLANE
ROAD	GAGE

Puzzle 94

TRAVEL NUMBER SEQUENCE

Nick is having to queue up for a new passport as he wants to travel. There are a lot of people in front of him, each with their own numbered ticket. Nick notices the numbers they have been given form a pattern. Can you work out what it is, and what the next number will be?

Puzzle 95

WINTER GEAR WORDS

Your ski holiday suitcase has spilled in the forest and Grand Pabbie the rock troll has found what was in there. He won't return everything unless you can tell him precisely the name of each item. Can you name the items from the clues? Then Pabbie will let you get on with your vacation!

To help, Pabbie has told you the number of letters in each word!

1. Cover your feet with these woolly: (5)
2. Don't get sunburned, use: (8)
3. Go fast downhill on these: (4)
4. Keep your neck warm with a: (5)
5. Protect your body from the cold: (6)
6. These are special ski trousers: (10)
7. To keep your hands warm and dry: (6)
8. To protect your eyes: (7)
9. Wear this on your head: (6)
10. Footwear for skiing: (5)

Puzzle 96

HOOK'S DARK SHADOW

That naughty Captain Hook is always causing trouble in his quest to take revenge on Peter Pan. The boys of Neverland are always on the lookout for Hook and his crew, even when they're on holiday. Each silhouettes opposite has one small difference from the original. Can you circle the difference in each image?

Puzzle 97

TRAIN TRACKS

Casey Junior travels through day and night, carrying Dumbo and the circus across the country. He has plenty of time to think, and he has come up with a logic puzzle for his friends to solve.

In the grid below, the numbers across the top and side tell you the number of squares that have train tracks in them for each column and row respectively. You have to work out the path of the single railway track all the way from A to B. Tracks may only be straight or 90-degree curved (as shown), and the track may not cross over itself anywhere.

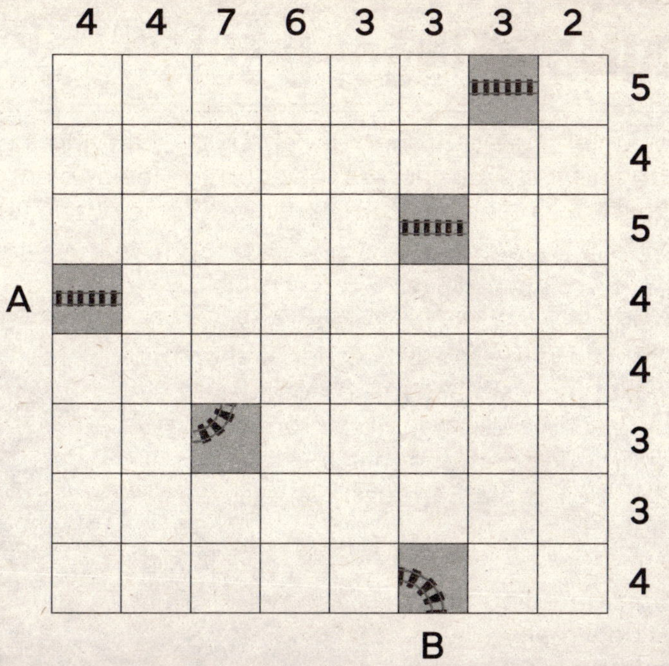
4 4 7 6 3 3 3 2
5
4
5
A
4
4
3
3
4
B

Puzzle 98

FRIENDLY SUDOKU SUMS

Baloo and Mowgli are planning a jungle adventure but they have a few sums to do before they leave.

Each row and column on the grid must contain the numbers 1, 2, 3, 4 and 5 once only. Additionally, the arithmetic clues must be correct (the number in the top left corner of each thick box must be possible to make from the numbers within each thick box from the arithmetic operation that is shown, for example '5+' must **add** up to 5).

The highlighted number shows how many nights Baloo and Mowgli plan to spend on their jungle tour!

2-		2÷		5+
2÷	2-	5x		
		9+	6x	10+
2÷				
20x		2-		

Puzzle 99

BEACH LOGIC

Moana is playing on the island with her little sister Simea, and Pua and Heihei. The four of them race across the beach, gathering shells as they go. From the clues below, can you work out the order they finished in, and how many shells each player gathered during the race?

Use the clues to put a tick or cross in the grid, then use logic to work out what you are missing.

The racer who finished first gathered more shells than Heihei.

Simea gathered 10 shells.

Heihei ended the race in second place.

Pua gathered 1 less shell than the person who ended the race in third place.

Moana gathered 13 shells and did not come first.

		Number of shells				Race position			
		10	11	12	13	First	Second	Third	Fourth
Name	Pua								
	Moana								
	Heihei								
	Simea								
Race position	First								
	Second								
	Third								
	Fourth								

Puzzle 100

TEN DISNEY QUESTIONS

To finish, we've set up a final quiz, all about names and places. Caution: these questions are tough!

1. What does Moana's name mean in several Polynesian languages?

2. What are the names of the nine lands found at Disneyland?

3. Which villain says, 'We were so close! So close, we tripped at the finish line!'?

4. In *Up*, where does Charles Muntz live?

5. Where do the trolls in *Frozen* live?

6. In *The Lion King*, where does Rafiki draw a picture of Simba?

7. In *The Black Cauldron*, what are the names of The Witches of Morva?

8. What does Aurora mean in Latin?

9. In *Sleeping Beauty*, where is Maleficent's lair located?

10. In *Zootopia*, what town is Judy Hopps from?

The Answers

Puzzle 1

RAYA'S BEACH CROSSING

Puzzle 2

TIANA'S TIME OUT

L	A	G	O	O	N	T	C	E	N
I	R	S	U	R	F	I	N	G	B
G	F	S	E	E	A	D	S	O	U
H	T	L	N	A	T	E	P	C	C
T	E	O	I	O	S	C	A	E	K
H	B	K	W	P	R	H	D	A	E
O	E	A	A	E	P	K	E	N	T
U	A	Y	V	P	L	E	E	L	P
S	C	A	E	A	J	B	R	L	L
E	H	K	S	B	O	O	K	S	C

Puzzle 3

ARIEL'S SUDOKU SECRET

1	4	2	3
3	2	4	1
4	3	1	2
2	1	3	4

Puzzle 4

TOULOUSE IN TIME?

No they won't. The carriage will take 30 minutes so they will be ten minutes late.

Puzzle 5

ABUELA'S HOUSE INSPECTION

1 ↘	12 ↓	9 ↙	4 ↙
11 ↗	13 ↓	3 ↗	8 ↖
10 ↑	6 →	2 ↑	7 ↑
5 ↗	14 →	1 →	16 ¤

Puzzle 6

FIND NEMO'S HOME!

LOST

HOST

HOSE

HOME

Puzzle 7

SUM SUDOKU WITH SARGE

4x 1	5+ 3	2	2÷ 4
4	2÷ 1	1- 3	2
5+ 3	2	4	2- 1
2	4x 4	1	3

Puzzle 8
COMPARING POCAHONTAS

Puzzle 9
MOANA'S OCEAN MATHEMATICS

3	+	5	-	8	=	0
+		-		-		
9	+	2	-	6	=	5
-		+		+		
1	+	4	-	7	=	-2
=		=		=		
11		7		9		

Puzzle 10
AURORA'S WAKE-UP CALL

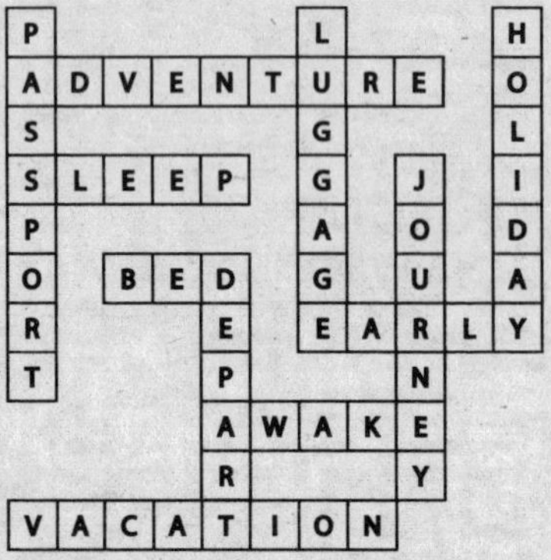

Puzzle 12
CINDERELLA'S RIDDLE

The letter 'A'.

Puzzle 13
A DIFFERENT BELLE

Puzzle 14

FRIENDS IN ORDER

Happy is at the front, Doc is in the middle, Sleepy is at the back.

Puzzle 15

EVE'S WORD MATCH

1d, 2a, 3h, 4e, 5c, 6g, 7b, 8f.

Puzzle 16

TEN DISNEY QUESTIONS

1. True, 2. b, 3. d, 4. c, 5. a, 6. a, 7. a, 8. a, 9. False. He is talking to Buzz, 10. a

Puzzle 17

WORD FINDER BAYMAX

1. Crab, 2. Cake, 3. Race, 4. Crate, 5. Racket, 6. Creaky, 7. Bicker, 8. Rickety, 9. Cart, 10. Brick

Puzzle 18

LIGHTNING'S FAST FILL UP!

FUME
FUMY
FURY
FURL
FULL

Puzzle 19

MERIDA'S FOREST FOOTPATH

Puzzle 20

JASMINE'S CALCULATIONS

9	-	5	+	3	=	7
+		-		-		
8	+	4	-	2	=	10
-		-		+		
6	-	1	+	7	=	12
=		=		=		
11		0		8		

Puzzle 21

PETER, THE LOST BOYS, AND NUMBERS

1 is added to the first number, then 2, then 3, so it increases by 1 each time.

The next number in the sequence is 22 (16 + 6).

Puzzle 23
STARFISH AND STONES WITH ALBERTO

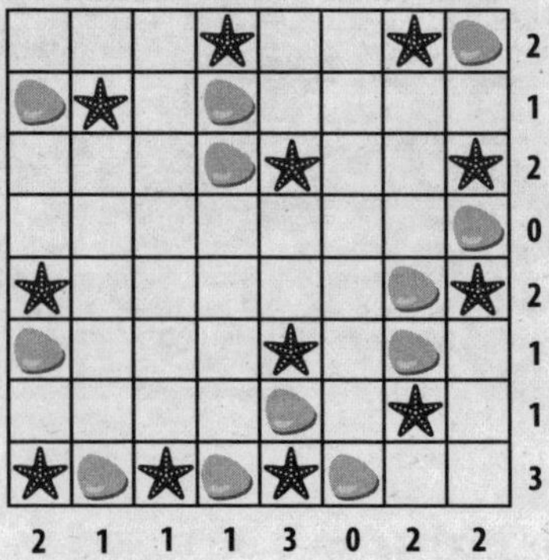

Puzzle 24
ANDY'S ABSENCE PUZZLE

		P	L	A	Y	T	I	M	E
U			E			O			
N			A	N	D	Y			
I			V			S			
V			I			T			C
E			N		L	O	T	S	O
R			G			R			L
S						Y			L
I				R					E
T	R	A	V	E	L	L	I	N	G
Y				X					E

Puzzle 25
RIDDLE ME BAD
A cherry

Puzzle 26
MADRIGAL FAMILY WORDSEARCH

W	S	O	N	G	S	F	O	R	K
S	A	C	H	A	I	R	S	I	O
L	A	T	I	B	Z	Y	D	U	U
C	E	L	E	B	R	A	T	E	T
V	F	M	A	R	O	H	G	E	D
D	A	K	O	D	M	V	R	A	O
R	M	N	S	N	R	E	I	T	O
I	I	I	I	T	A	B	L	E	R
N	L	F	S	G	K	D	L	O	S
K	Y	E	P	L	A	T	E	S	N

Puzzle 27
SWEEPING UP!

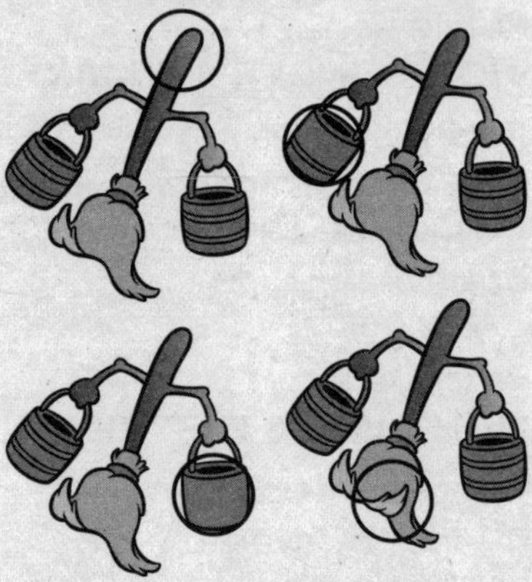

Puzzle 28
WHERE FOR WADE AND EMBER?
Ember opposite Wade
Bernie opposite Brook
Brook on Ember's left;
Bernie on Ember's right

Puzzle 29
BO PEEP'S WORD ROUNDUP
Barcelona, Spain
Cancun, Mexico
Dublin, Ireland
Hamburg, Germany
Miami, USA
Marseille, France
Rome, Italy
Stockholm, Sweden
Edinburgh, Scotland
Tokyo, Japan

Puzzle 30
TEN DISNEY QUESTIONS
1. Her father's hat, 2. a.
3. False, he is taught by Remy, who is a rat,
4. Charles F. Muntz, 5. c,
6. The Cave of Wonders, 7. c,
8. c, 9. c, 10. b.

Puzzle 31
WORD FINDER 22
1. Vet, 2. Cave, 3. Oven,
4. Vine, 5. Coven, 6. Movie,
7. Vitamin, 8. Invite,
9. Vietnam, 10. Inactive

Puzzle 32
LUCA'S START CALCULATOR

2	3	1	4
4	1	3	2
3	4	2	1
1	2	4	3

Puzzle 33
SUDOKU SUMS WITH WINNIE THE POOH

1- 2	4+ 3	4x 1	4
3	1	1- 4	2÷ 2
8x 4	2	3	2- 1
10+ 1	4	2	3

Puzzle 34
WORD MATCHING WITH LILO
1h, 2f, 3e, 4i, 5g, 7c, 6b, 8a, 9j.

Puzzle 35
DUMBO DIFFERENCE

Puzzle 36

BASIL AND THE CASE OF THE MISSING LETTERS

BRAZIL, GREECE, ITALY, MALAYSIA, MEXICO, SOUTH KOREA, SOUTH AFRICA, THAILAND, UNITED KINGDOM, UNITED STATES

Puzzle 37

FINDING THE INVISIBLE GIRL

1 ↘	12 ↓	11 ←	7 ↙
9 →	2 →	10 ↑	3 ↙
14 ↘	13 ←	4 ↓	6 ↑
8 ↑	15 →	5 ↗	16 ¤

Puzzle 38

QUASIMODO'S SPARROW SEQUENCE

The next number is 120. The pattern starts at 1 and multiplies first by two, then increasing by one each time (x2, x3, and so on).

Puzzle 39

DESERT WORD FINDER

1. Dunes, 2. Cactus, 3. Oasis, 4. Sahara Desert, 5. Sandstorm, 6. Mirage, 7. Camel, 8. Drought, 9. Sunburn, 10. Refreshing

Puzzle 40

BUG PLACEMENT WITH PRINCESS ATTA

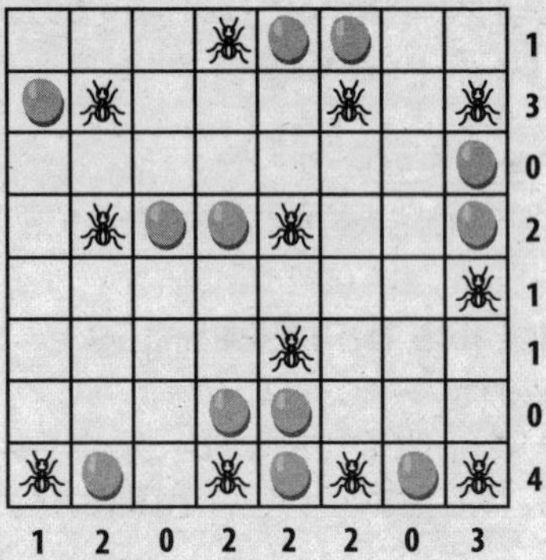

Puzzle 41

FLEEING WITH FLYNN

Five hours: one hour at 6 km/h (6km), one hour at 5 km/h (11km), and three at 3 km/h (20km).

Puzzle 42

MEI'S SUDOKU SHOW

6	2	5	3	1	4
4	1	3	5	6	2
1	4	2	6	3	5
5	3	6	2	4	1
2	6	1	4	5	3
3	5	4	1	2	6

Puzzle 43

JUDY'S CROSS-TOWN MAZE

Puzzle 44

FELINE DIFFERENCES

Puzzle 45

SEARCH WITH STITCH

Puzzle 46

CAPITAL CITY CHALLENGE

Australia: Canberra
Red herring: Sydney
Brazil: Brasilia
Red herring: Rio de Janeiro
Canada: Ottawa
Red herring: Toronto
France: Paris
Germany: Berlin
India: New Delhi
Red Herring: Mumbai
Mexico: Mexico City
United States: Washington, D.C.
Red herring: New York
United Kingdom: London
Thailand: Bangkok

Puzzle 47

MEMORIES MAP

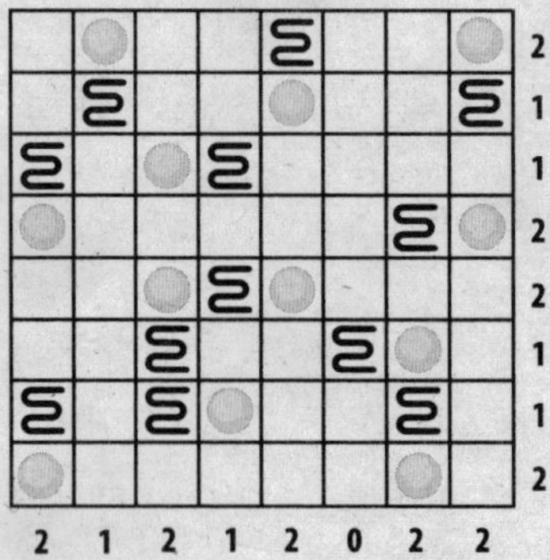

Puzzle 49

ANGER'S ARITHMETIC SUDOKU

7+ 4	2- 3	2	2÷ 1
3	2÷ 1	6+ 2	4
1- 1	2	4	3x 3
2	12x 4	3	1

Puzzle 50

SILHOUETTE ROUND-UP

Puzzle 51

JUST CHECKING THE NUMBERS!

8	+	1	+	3	=	12
+		+		-		
7	+	4	-	2	=	9
-		+		+		
9	+	5	-	6	=	8
=		=		=		
6		10		7		

Puzzle 52

ANCIENT WORLD MATCHUP

1e, 2f, 3i, 4a, 5g, 6c, 7d, 8h, 9b, 10j.

Puzzle 53

CROSSTOWN TRAFFIC

Fred's shortcut is the quickest (28 minutes). Go Go Tomago's maglev disks will take 40 minutes, the battle-bot will take 30 minutes.

Puzzle 54
JOY'S PUZZLED FEELINGS
An emoji.

Puzzle 55
WHATEVER NEXT!
11. It's the next prime number (only divisible by 1 and itself).

Puzzle 56
SLING YOUR HOOK

1 ↓	8 ↘	11 ↙	10 ←
5 ↘	12 ↘	9 ↗	15 ↓
4 ↑	3 ←	13 →	14 ↑
2 ↗	7 ↑	6 ←	16 ¤

Puzzle 57
JASMINE'S JOURNEY
SAND
SANE
SAME
SOME
HOME

Puzzle 58
TEN DISNEY QUESTIONS
1. Cogsworth is a clock, 2. Fear Tech, 3. Mickey's sorcerer's hat, 4. d, 5. London, 6. Motunui, 7. Regent's Park in London, UK, 8. d, 9. The Axiom, 10. The Spirit of Adventure

Puzzle 59
URSULA'S LOGICAL SEARCH

		Places			Objects		
		Market	Grotto	Palace	Trident	Fish	Ship
Names	Sebastian	✗	✗	✓	✗	✗	✓
	Flounder	✓	✗	✗	✗	✓	✗
	Scuttle	✗	✓	✗	✓	✗	✗
Objects	Trident	✗	✓	✗			
	Fish	✓	✗	✗			
	Ship	✗	✗	✓			

Puzzle 60
MONSTER WORD GRID

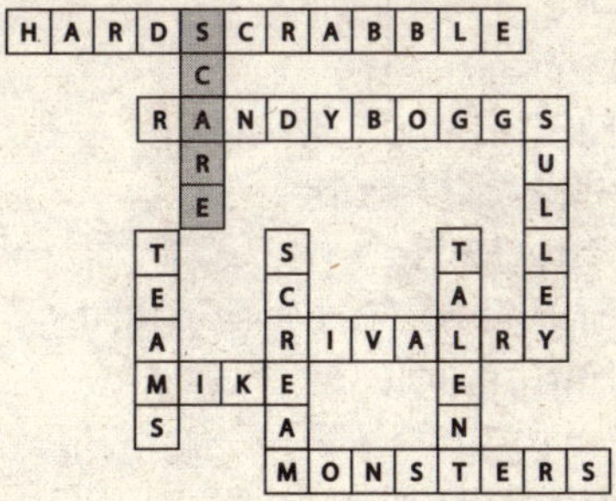

Puzzle 61
FROZEN RIVER CROSSING

Puzzle 62
LOCKER CODE SUDOKU

5	1	4	6	3	2
6	3	3	4	5	1
4	6	1	5	2	3
3	2	5	1	4	6
1	5	3	2	6	4
2	4	6	3	1	5

Puzzle 63
DRIVEN TO DISTRACTION

Beach: Relaxing, Sunbathe, Watersports
Mountain: Climbing, Hiking, Nature
City: Museums, Sightseeing, Monuments
Safari: Animals, Habitat, Savannah
Theme Park: Rides, Thrills, Rollercoaster

Puzzle 64
ALICE AT THE FAIR

It's a case of Tweedledum's bad calculation. In fact, they spent £27: £25 on the entrance fee, £2 on sweets and they received £3 back, equalling £30.

Puzzle 65
KRISTOFF'S WARM WORDSEARCH

F	R	O	Z	E	N	X	E	S	C	P	A	C	I	T
P	M	M	H	O	T	C	H	O	C	O	L	A	T	E
L	Z	M	I	S	S	Q	O	K	T	Y	Y	B	D	V
R	S	X	S	Z	L	L	J	M	I	I	D	I	I	R
G	B	N	D	K	V	K	E	F	D	C	K	N	G	W
O	I	S	O	M	A	F	J	I	U	E	T	S	S	S
G	K	E	S	W	I	T	P	V	G	R	S	N	N	N
G	Q	L	H	G	M	T	I	L	I	H	K	O	O	O
L	C	R	S	L	F	A	T	N	H	V	I	W	W	W
E	H	I	L	A	R	C	N	E	G	J	I	B	B	F
S	A	G	E	C	O	O	T	Z	N	C	N	O	A	L
N	L	L	D	I	S	Z	C	D	R	S	G	A	L	A
B	E	O	K	E	T	Y	S	C	A	R	F	R	L	K
U	T	O	X	R	U	P	H	X	A	I	I	D	M	E
K	P	F	I	R	E	P	L	A	C	E	O	D	H	V

Puzzle 66
OBSERVE THE DIFFERENCE

Puzzle 67
HERCULES' HEAVY PYRAMID

485
211 274
87 124 150
36 51 73 77
17 19 32 41 36
10 7 12 20 21 15
7 3 4 8 12 9 6

Puzzle 68
THE QUEEN'S CONUNDRUM
47 cards (5 missing from a deck of 52).
With three people they get 15 cards each and 2 remain.
With four people they get 11 cards each and 3 remain.
With five people they get 9 cards each and 2 remain.

Puzzle 69
SUDOKU WITH SUMS

5x 5	12x 3	5+ 4	1	1- 2
1	4	3- 5	2	3
3x 3	1	6+ 2	1- 4	5
10x 2	5	1	3	5+ 4
2÷ 4	2	2- 3	5	1

Puzzle 70
PUPPY PURSUIT

1 →	11 ↙	14 ↘	2 ↙
12 →	13 ↗	7 ↓	15 ↓
9 →	6 ↗	8 ←	10 ↖
3 →	5 ↑	4 ←	16 ¤

Puzzle 71
TURN UP THE HEAT
FIRE, HIRE, HERE, HERD, HEAD, HEAT

Puzzle 72
GODS OF OLYMPUS
Starting from Hercules and moving clockwise to his left, they are seated in the following order: Hercules–Hera–Meg–Pegasus–Zeus.

Puzzle 73
UNDER SEA SILHOUETTE

Puzzle 74

WOODY'S WORD WHEEL

1. AEROPLANE, 2. PIRATE, 3. TAPIR, 4. APRIL, 5. PLANET, 6. REPLAN, 7. PAINTER, 8. TRAIN, 9. LEAP, 10. NAP

Puzzle 75

HONEY TIME

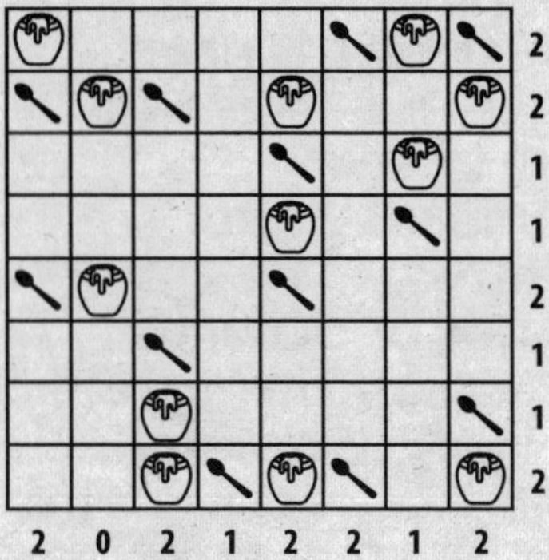

Puzzle 77

SEALIFE WITH DORY

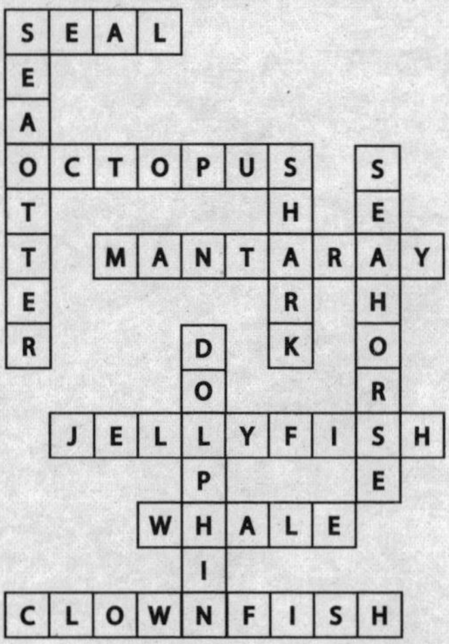

Puzzle 78

WATERY WORD MATCH

Arctic Ocean
Atlantic Ocean
Bering Sea
Black Sea
Caribbean Sea
Caspian Sea
Indian Ocean
Mediterranean Sea
North Sea
Pacific Ocean
Persian Gulf
Red Sea
Sargasso Sea
South China Sea
Yellow Sea

Puzzle 79

TEN DISNEY QUESTIONS

1. Bald Mountain, 2. Hungary, 3. New York City, 4. Morro Bay, California, 5. c, 6. The North Mountain, 7. d, 8. Route 66, 9. The hyenas, 10. Nomanisan Island

Puzzle 80

RIDDLE TIME

1. A clock
2. A palindrome (a word which reads the same forwards and backwards, for example, the words civic and madam).
3. The letter 'e'

Puzzle 81
THE CAVE OF WONDERS

1 ↘	10 ↙	4 ↙	17 ↙	16 ←
11 ↓	5 ↘	3 ↑	14 →	15 ↑
12 ↓	21 ↓	2 ↑	8 ↘	7 ←
18 ↘	22 →	23 ↓	6 ↗	9 ↖
13 ↗	19 →	24 →	20 ↖	25 ¤

Puzzle 82
MEDITERRANEAN SPELLING MAZE

Puzzle 83
WORDSEARCH WISHES

Puzzle 84
JUNGLE MATHS

7	+	8	-	9	=	6
+		+		-		
1	+	2	-	3	=	0
-		-		+		
6	+	5	-	4	=	7
=		=		=		
2		5		10		

Puzzle 85
WALL·E WORDS

1. Waste Allocation Load Lifter: Earth-class
2. One
3. Extraterrestrial Vegetation Evaluer
4. A cockroach
5. The twenty-ninth century
6. A seedling
7. M-O (Microbe-Obliterator)
8. Captain B. McCrea
9. AUTO

Puzzle 86

WORK WORD LADDER

WORK, FORK, FORM, FOAM, FLAM, FLAY, PLAY

Puzzle 87

DOG GONE

Puzzle 88

WHERE ON EARTH?

ASPEN (USA)
BANFF (Canada)
CHAMONIX (France)
CANARY ISLANDS (Spain)
MOUNT FUJI (Japan)
REYKJAVIK (Iceland)
TALLINN (Estonia)
TROMSO (Norway)
WHISTLER (Canada)
ZERMATT (Swizerland)

Puzzle 89

LOGICAL EMOTIONS

		Destination			Arrived		
		Alaska	Hawaii	New York	First	Second	Third
Names	Joy	✗	✓	✗	✓	✗	✗
	Anxiety	✗	✗	✓	✗	✓	✗
	Disgust	✓	✗	✗	✗	✗	✓
Arrived	First	✗	✓	✗			
	Second	✗	✗	✓			
	Third	✓	✗	✗			

Puzzle 90

JIGSAW PUZZLER

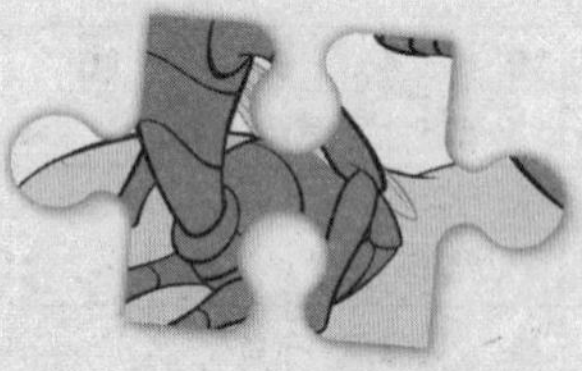

Puzzle 91

COCO CROSSWORD

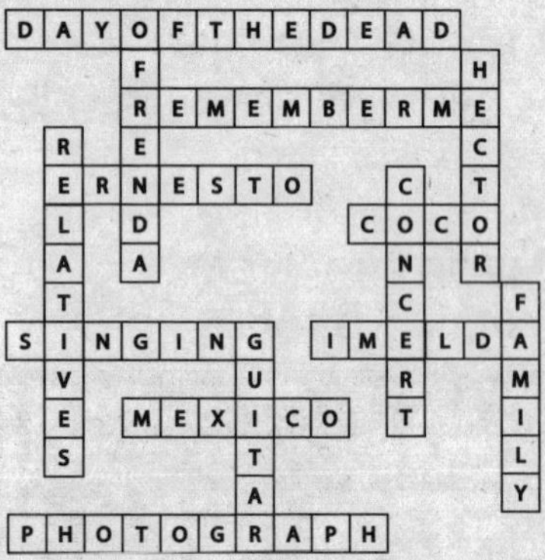

Puzzle 92

SUDOKU REVEALER

5	2	4	9	1	6	8	7	3
8	3	7	5	2	4	9	6	1
1	6	9	8	7	3	5	4	2
2	7	5	4	9	1	3	8	6
3	9	1	6	8	2	7	5	4
4	8	6	3	5	7	1	2	9
6	5	8	2	3	9	4	1	7
7	4	9	1	6	5	2	9	8
9	1	2	7	4	8	6	3	5

Puzzle 93

MAGIC MIRROR JUMBLE

SUNCREAM, SUITCASE, LUGGAGE, BACKPACK, RUCKSACK, PASSPORT, SEASIDE, AIRPLANE, LIFEGUARD, ROAD TRIP

Puzzle 94

TRAVEL NUMBER SEQUENCE

61. The sequence starts with 1, then follows a pattern of x2 then +3.

Puzzle 95

WINTER GEAR WORDS

1. Socks, 2. Suncream, 3. Skis, 4. Scarf, 5. Jacket, 6. Salopettes, 7. Gloves, 8. Goggles, 9. Helmet, 10. Boots

Puzzle 96

HOOK'S DARK SHADOW

Puzzle 97

TRAIN TRACKS

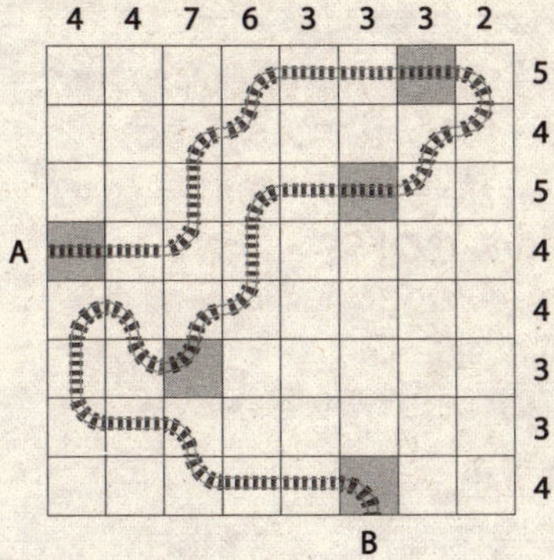

Puzzle 98

FRIENDLY SUDOKU SUMS

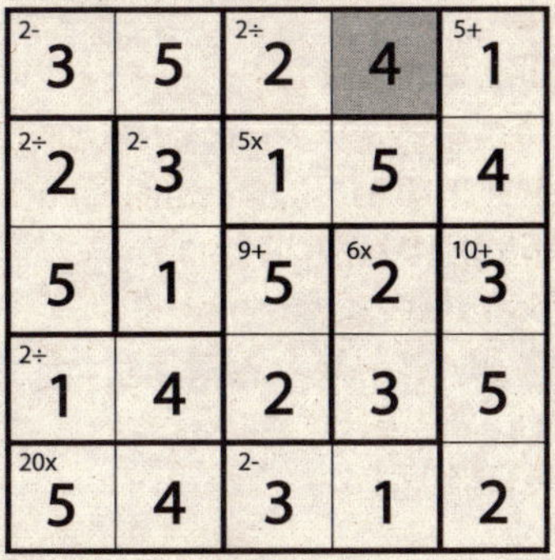

2- 3	5	2÷ 2	4	5+ 1
2÷ 2	2- 3	5x 1	5	4
5	1	9+ 5	6x 2	10+ 3
2÷ 1	4	2	3	5
20x 5	4	2- 3	1	2

Puzzle 99

BEACH LOGIC

		Number of shells				Race position			
		10	11	12	13	First	Second	Third	Fourth
Name	Pua	✘	✘	✔	✘	✔	✘	✘	✘
	Moana	✘	✘	✘	✔	✘	✘	✔	✘
	Heihei	✘	✔	✘	✘	✘	✔	✘	✘
	Simea	✔	✘	✘	✘	✘	✘	✘	✔
Race position	First	✘	✘	✔	✘				
	Second	✔	✘	✘	✘				
	Third	✘	✘	✘	✔				
	Fourth	✘	✔	✘	✘				

Puzzle 100

TEN DISNEY QUESTIONS

1. Ocean,
2. Adventureland, Critter Country, Fantasyland, Frontierland, Main Street, USA, Mickey's Toontown, New Orleans Square, Star Wars: Galaxy's Edge and Tomorrowland.
3. Hades in Hercules
4. In a cave
5. Valley of the Living Rock
6. The Tree of Life
7. Orddu, Orgoch and Orwen
8. Dawn
9. The Forbidden Mountains
10. Bunnyburrow

Use this page to work out your answers

Use this page to work out your answers

Use this page to work out your answers

Use this page to work out your answers

Use this page to work out your answers

Use this page to work out your answers

Use this page to work out your answers

Use this page to work out your answers

Use this page to work out your answers

Use this page to work out your answers

Use this page to work out your answers